W9-AWF-116

A JUST FOR A DAY BOOK

LIZARD IN THE SUN

JOANNE RYDER

ILLUSTRATED BY

MICHAEL ROTHMAN

A MULBERRY PAPERBACK BOOK / NEW YORK

For Gabriel and Esteban Salinas with love
J.R.

To Dorothy and Bernie Schursky
M.R.

Special thanks to James P. O'Brien of the Department of Herpetology, California Academy of Sciences, for his expert reading of the manuscript.

AUTHOR'S NOTE

The green anole (*Anolis carolinensis*) known as the "American chameleon" lives in the southeastern United States and is a common pet. Like all lizards, anoles are cold-blooded animals. Their body temperature matches closely the temperature of their surroundings. If it is cool, anoles are cool and sluggish. They can warm themselves by basking in the sun. When the temperature is warm, they are warm and active.

While the anole is not a true chameleon, it shares with chameleons the trait of rapidly changing the color of its skin. Though it is generally supposed that chameleons and anoles change color in order to camouflage with their surroundings, this is not true.

A complex variety of factors—including changes in temperature, light, and their emotional state—produce the quick, involuntary color changes in anoles. Sometimes their skin color may, by chance, blend in with their surroundings and serve to camouflage them from hungry predators, but not always. And two anoles may be seen in the same spot—one bright green and the other brown.

Male anoles have large, brightly colored throat fans which they display to defend their territories and to court females. During displays, they bob their heads while doing push-ups.

Text copyright © 1990 by Joanne Ryder
Illustrations copyright © 1990 by Michael Rothman
All rights reserved.
No part of this book by be reproduced or utilized in any form
or by any means, electronic or mechanical, including photocopying and recording,
or by any information storage and retrieval system, without permission in writing
from the Publisher. Inquiries should be addressed to William Morrow & Company, Inc.,
1350 Avenue of the Americas, New York, New York 10019.

Printed in the United States of America.
First Mulberry Edition, 1994.

3 5 7 9 10 8 6 4 2

Library of Congress Cataloging-in-Publication Data
Ryder, Joanne.
Lizard in the sun / Joanne Ryder; illustrated by Michael Rothman.
p. cm.
Summary: A child is transformed into an anole for a day and
discovers what it is like to be a tiny lizard changing color
in a sunny, leafy world.
ISBN 0-688-13081-X
[1. Anoles—Fiction.] I. Rothman, Michael, ill. II. Title.
PZ7.R959Li 1990
[E]—dc20 89-33886 CIP AC

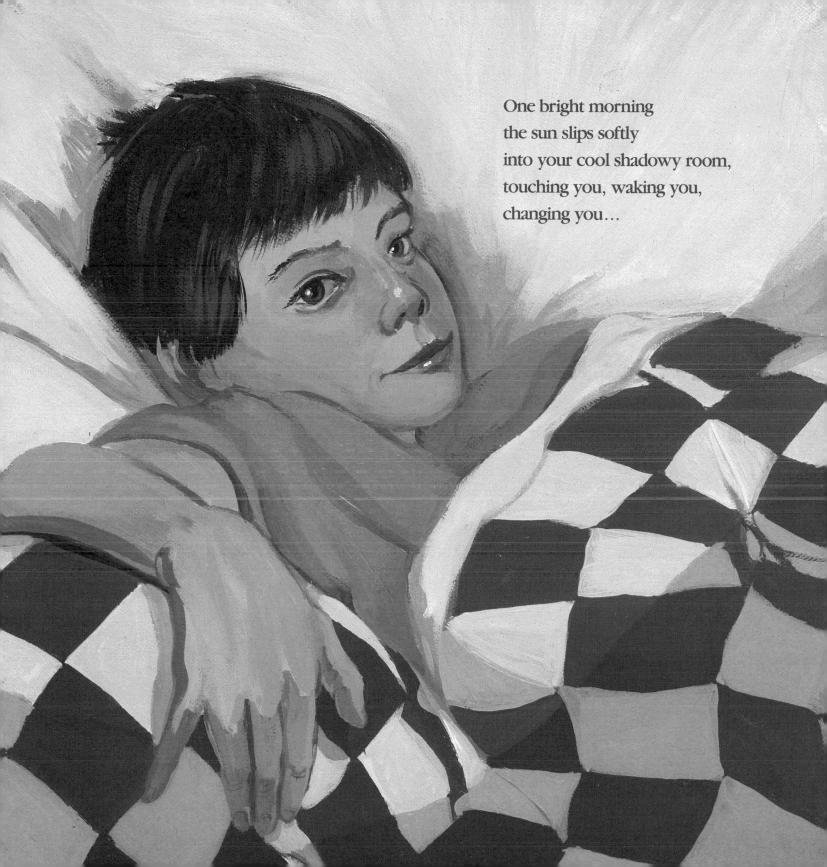

One bright morning
the sun slips softly
into your cool shadowy room,
touching you, waking you,
changing you…

till you feel yourself
growing smaller and smaller.
You are a lizard, small and thin,
as light as a pencil,
as light as a handful of popcorn.

Still cool and sleepy,
you slide off your soft bed,
landing…
on four brown feet!
The thick rug tickles
your thin tan belly
as you creep,
your long brown tail
trailing behind.

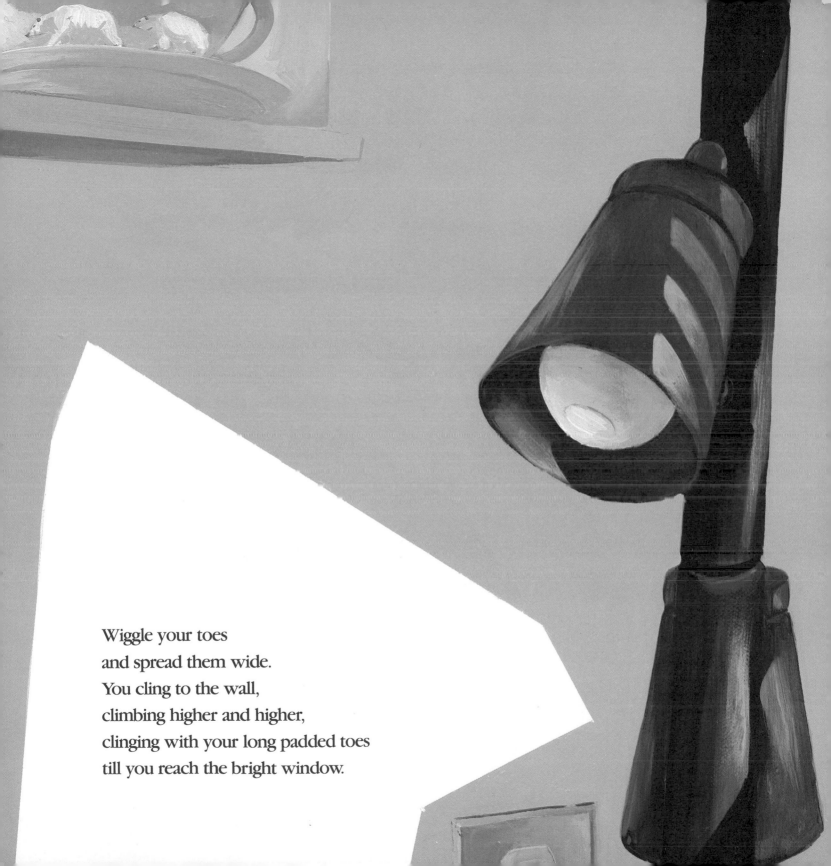

Wiggle your toes
and spread them wide.
You cling to the wall,
climbing higher and higher,
clinging with your long padded toes
till you reach the bright window.

There, you lie in the sun,
feeling its warmth wake you,
feeling the hot sunlight creep
along your scaly body.
In the warm sun
you change again....

Lean green lizard,
you feel the sun
singing inside you
and you run....
Dashing down a hot wall,
you leap into the bushes.
You run from one branch to the next—
a jungle of leaves flashes by you—
and you rest tucked inside a bush.

You are green
like the green leaves
all around you.
Someone hungry flies
over the green bushes,
over the green grass
and does not see you
in your pale green skin!

You are lean and green
and you leap
to a white sunny wall.
This is your world
and it feels good to
be a lizard in the sun.
You bob your head
up and down.
Like a tiny athlete,
you push up and down
on your strong green legs.

Your throat fans out wide
and changes color!
Red…red…red…
your bright throat flashes.
You are proud,
telling all who see you
you are a lizard
and this is *your* spot in the sun.

You are lean and green
and hungry.
Bzzzzzz bzzzzzz…
You creep closer and catch
the whirring fly
snap snap
in your wide fast mouth.

You are lean and green
and thirsty.
Long leaves curl
and make a tiny pool of water.
You drink, licking the water
with your thin pink tongue.

You climb
up the tall fence
and rest in the sunlight,
feeling warm and good.
Brownness creeps
along your scaly back
and you rest like a dark twig
fallen on the old fence.

On this bright day
you rest, then run
and catch your food
in your wide fast mouth.
And now
you are lean and green,
and now
you are brown,
and now
you are in between!
Sometimes you match
the greenness, the brownness
around you.
Sometimes you don't.

Slowly, the hot sun sinks down
behind the trees, behind the bushes
and you can feel coolness
creep along your quick legs,
your flat head,
your lean back,
your thin tail.

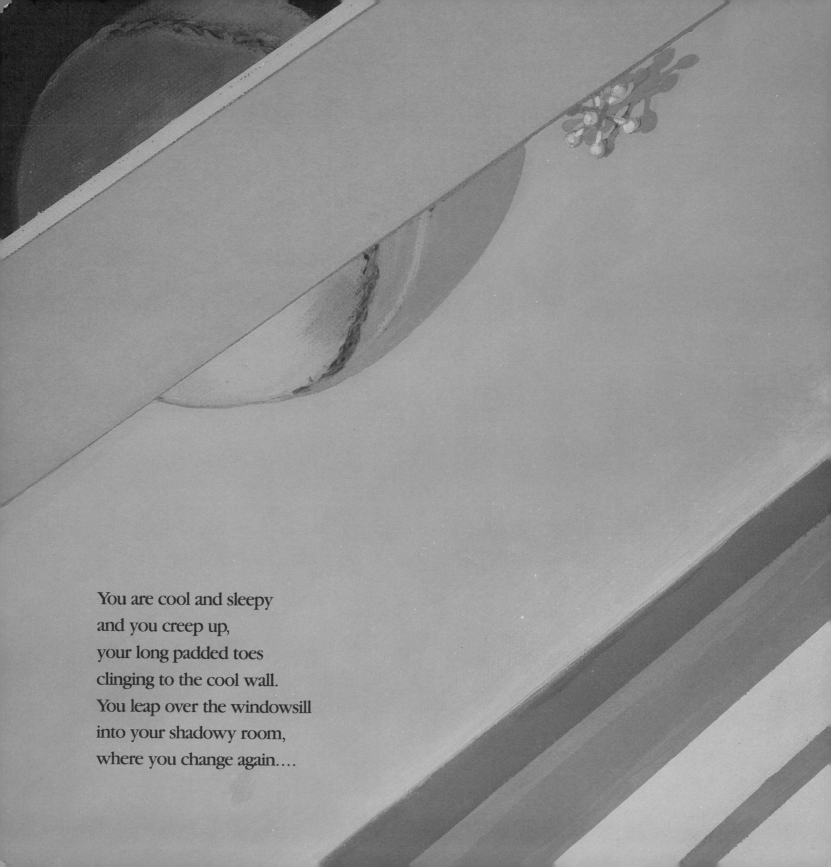

You are cool and sleepy
and you creep up,
your long padded toes
clinging to the cool wall.
You leap over the windowsill
into your shadowy room,
where you change again....

And there you find
a good place to rest
after your long day in the sun.